DIY Book Promo:

How to Find Readers Without Spending Money

Dan Klefstad

A CIP catalogue record for this book is
available from the British Library
ISBN: 978-1739367541

Typeset in **Garamond**

*This publication is designated to provide competent and
reliable information regarding the subject matter covered.
However, it is sold with the understanding that the
author and publisher are not engaged in rendering legal,
financial, or other professional advice. Laws and
practices often vary from state to state and country to
country and if legal or other expert assistance is required,
the services of a professional should be sought. The
author and publisher specifically disclaim any liability
that is incurred from the use of application of the contents
of this book.*

www.BurtonMayersBooks.com

DEDICATION

To all the published authors trying to stand out
in this crowded market.

CONTENTS

ACKNOWLEDGMENTS

Thanks to Richard Mayers at Burton Mayers Books for agreeing to release this, my second BMB title.

Thanks to Stephen Zimmer and Holly Phillippe for inviting me to present "DIY Book Promo" at the Imaginarium Convention. Your invitation prompted me to write this book!

Special thanks to Susan for her love and patience.

FOREWORD BY WC TURCK

Are you ready for an astounding and historic statement? According to the online publisher Bowker, self-published books now consistently outperform the larger, or vanity presses in sales. Selfpublishingadvice.org reported the "global printing industry is forecast to reach $821 billion by 2022, driven by digital and POD printing." Independent and self-published authors now account for as much as 34 percent of all e-book sales, again in data from selfpublishingadvice.org. The online big data site, Statista.com reports that global book sales rose from $122billion USD in 2018 to $129billion USD. Wordsrated.com reports that 300 million self-published books are sold annually.

The marketplace opportunities for indie and self-published authors to reach a truly global audience has never been greater. To put that in a clearer perspective, there are roughly 4.7 billion internet users worldwide, of which only about 500 million speak English as their first language, or less than 20 percent. There are definite opportunities to getting your book in the hands of readers. On the other hand, that creates a challenging marketplace in making any book stand out amid those daunting numbers.

Self-promotion and book marketing are virtually anathema to most authors. Ours is a solitary effort to tell our stories through an ever-widening mastery of the word, the sentence, the paragraph. We exalt in the solemn solitude of hours spent weighing the rhythm and precise intention of our narrative and prose. It is Art, and there is no small amount of religiosity in that eternal and deeply personal expression. The crass reality of business branding and marketing of that work is perceived all too often as an affront to that sublime expression.

As an author and the host of Chicago Writes, the podcast of the Chicago Writer's Association, I actively engaged guests and authors about book marketing strategies. Indeed, the topic is so big, so complex, and so imperative to Authors that the topic frequently occupies whole programs. It need not be a minefield, fraught with scams, discouragement, or a wasteful money pit. That doesn't need to be the case, though those minefields continue to prey upon many unsuspecting authors. A look at that marketplace helps us to understand.

Self-publishing is as old as writing itself. *Republic*, the seminal work by the Greek Philosopher Plato (424/423 – 348 BC), was self-published. So was *Metamorphoses* by the exiled Augustan dissenting poet Ovid (21 March 43 BC – AD 17/18). Thomas Paine's rhetorical polemic against the Crown of England, *Common Sense*, was self-published in 1775. Writing as a woman, Jane Austen was refused by contemporary British publishers forcing her to self-publish anonymously.

For the next several centuries authors went the so-called traditional route to publishing: pitch, submission, acceptance/rejection, publication. That served as a sort of quality control, but it also became a choke point inhibiting the democratization of information and the printed word. It all but guaranteed the hegemony of narrowed perspectives about knowledge, storytelling, and the fullest spectrum of the Human condition. Even the most egalitarian of publishers were forced to make marketing and financial decisions about who and what might be published. The personal computer and a hang-gliding enthusiast changed everything.

In 1973, a parachute company manager named Dan Poynter, took up hang gliding. Unable to find anything in print on the subject, Poynter literally wrote the book. That happened to coincide with the emergence of the word processor and personal computer. By the end of the decade Poynter published a how-to guide, titled *The Self-Publishing Manual: How to Write, Print, and Sell Your Own Book*. However, the cost of a personal computer, let alone self-publishing remained prohibitively expensive for most people until the mid-1990s. Those with the means to self-publish were forced to speculate at great financial risk without knowing whether they might ever see a return on investment for their pre-printed manuscripts.

Then, in the late 1990s publishing was forever changed by POD or print-on-demand books. POD liberated small publishers and independent authors from expensive outlays for pre-printed books -- money that could now be diverted to marketing and promotion services rather than printing and warehousing books which might never sell.

The industry, more or less, maintained pace with the emerging digital revolution. The digital age drove big data which ushered in the great democratization of media, books, and information. Mammoth chains like Borders and Barnes & Noble subsumed that marketplace, briefly eclipsing small and independent bookstores. The book market landscape was changing.

To call the digital age a revolution is almost an understatement, in the same way the discovery of fire, the establishment of settled farming communities or the Gutenberg Press were less a revolution as a foundational paradigm shift for Humanity. We can only shake our heads at the astounding speed of the digital paradigm shift. At the publication of this book the digital age is hardly thirty years old; the iPhone and Kindle Readers have only been around for less than 25 years. Social media, which had been around via primitive message boards since the 1970s, got its real start in 1997 with the launch of *Six Degrees*. When it ended in 2001 *Six Degrees* had more than three million users. Small by contemporary metrics, but social media showed it could be successful.

Six Degrees was replaced in 2002 by *Friendster* which allowed users to post and share photos, videos, and messages. Globally, however, internet accessibility was still relatively nascent, approaching an average of 16 percent of the population. That disparity was only slightly higher than the global rate of illiteracy at the time of the invention of Gutenberg's Press around 1455. According to the United Nations' International Telecommunication Union (ITU), within the span of five years the number of internet users worldwide grew to 30 percent, and by 2017 had risen to a meteoric 48 percent.

All the components for the self-publishing industry were coming together. The promise of connecting people worldwide saw the creation of *Myspace*, a template for a college meeting site, created, in part, by Mark Zuckerberg called *Facebook*. By 2009, *Facebook* had replaced *Myspace* as the number one visited internet site. As of 2023 *Facebook* boasts 2.6 billion active users worldwide. Virtually and digitally connecting roughly half of the planet's 63 percent, or 4.7 billion internet users. Don't worry, I'm building to what all this means for the independent author or publisher.

The other key component was a 1996 start up called *Amazon*. Strictly an online entity, *Amazon* allowed for the independent author and publishing houses to compete in the same virtual global marketplace as the large or vanity publishers. My first novel, *Broken, One Soldier's Unexpected Journey Home*, told the story of a young veteran suffering from PTSD, attempting to piece his life together through an old Ojibway Indian claiming to be a survivor of the wreck of the Edmund Fitzgerald. Despite the book's setting along the Lake Superior Shore, the book sold well in India and Northern Europe. That was due completely to the international reach of *Amazon*.

The opportunities for self-published authors are greater now than they ever were. The challenges of being seen or discovered in a global book marketplace are equally daunting. Book marketing is a patchwork. There are over-arching strategies for marketing a book, such as cover and book jacket design, pitch guidelines, demographic targeting, genre, etc. Within each genre-specific category there are finer points to consider. Action-adventure books must project insurmountable danger faced by a hero to reach its target audience. Romance stories should communicate passion, and a blushing sinfulness in a dramatic yet accessible setting. Non-fiction must communicate the experience and underlying expertise of the author, as well as the factual integrity of the subject matter. The Vampire fiction market is so over-saturated that it takes a truly unique vision to break through to readers, and always with a dark sensuality, like Dan Klefstad's *Fiona's Guardians*.

There are close to 4 million new book titles published each year, according to Tonerbuzz.com, 2.3 million were by self-published authors. All of this presents a mixed bag of opportunity and obstacle for the indie author. The key is to spotlight your product so that it stands out. Marketing can cost money, but this book offers important, real-life strategies in a very broad marketplace that the author has found worked for minimal or no outlay of your hard-earned cash. And make no mistake, the marketplace is filled with those ready to take the money from your pocket and leave you in the weeds.

Like Dan Klefstad, as a broadcaster I felt it was my mission to help fellow authors become more comfortable with broadcast interviews. This book offers valuable advice for a great opportunity to sell your book by directly speaking to your buyers. It also offers an important caution about interviews, and whether you should ever pay to be interviewed about your book.

I liken book marketing in this modern environment to attempting to dance on quicksand. Every independent author and publisher -- heck, even the large publishers -- are trying to figure out where to place resources and energy for a return on their publishing investment. It's all about getting your book in the hands of readers. We are all trying to find our way across that quicksand. Best to follow someone who has made it across a few times. This book is important in that regard.

WC Turck

DIY Book Promo

ABOUT THIS BOOK

Remember the Penguin Random House merger trial? In 2022, the U.S. Department of Justice sued to stop the company from acquiring Simon & Schuster, another Big Five publisher. The discovery process revealed a shocking fact, as revealed in this tweet:

> 8:05 PM 9/3/22
>
> OMG in the Penguin Random House/S&S antitrust trial it was revealed that out of 58,000 trade titles published per year, half of those titles sell fewer than one dozen books. LESS THAN ONE DOZEN.
>
> (reply to her own tweet) 90 percent of titles sell fewer than 2,000 units.

Most people saw the post and concluded the industry was dysfunctional and that publishing would always be unprofitable. I looked at it and thought, "What the hell are their authors doing? Shouldn't they spend more time promoting their books?"

No doubt, you detected the disdain of an indie author scarred by repeated rejection. I even got dumped by a publisher, meaning I had to start all over at the bottom of the ladder. Clawing up again, I found a new publisher who gave advice on how to find more readers. Not wanting to fail again, I continued climbing, eventually outselling many of my Big Five peers. But the more victories I grasped, the more tunneled my vision became, and suddenly I stopped noticing my fellow writers who slipped, fell off the ladder, and perished in obscurity. Finally, though, I reached a place where I felt safe enough to pause and look down at all those who sold just a handful of books. That's when it dawned on me: What if nobody told them they had to promote themselves? What if nobody taught them how to do it?

My fellow writers, it's time we shared what each of us has learned during our publishing and promoting journeys. My only request is that everything offered can be replicated or improved with a marketing budget of zero. This book contains every tool and trick I used during the three-year campaign for my novel, Fiona's Guardians. Steal whatever you want. Then tell me what worked for you at the next conference or book fest.

Who am I and why should you take my advice?

I recently retired from a 30-year career as a radio host and newscaster. Not surprisingly, much of my advice involves pitching media for interviews, performing well in an interview, and sharing that recording or article when it comes out.

This book contains every tool and trick I used during the three-year campaign for my vampire novel, Fiona's

Guardians. It's published by a small firm in the UK on what's often called a traditional contract. That means someone at the company liked my book enough to publish it and charged me nothing to bring it to market.

If you've heard of Fiona's Guardians, that's solid evidence of my promotional skills. Skip to the next chapter. If you haven't heard of my novel and need more convincing:

I got dozens of independent bookstores to order my novel *for their inventory* in addition to fulfilling customer requests.

The book was adapted by an all-professional acting company which converted several of my chapters into an episode of their Mysterious Journey podcast. It's available everywhere and it is excellent.

A short film adaptation is in pre-production. You'll find more on IMDB.

I've presented my DIY Book Promo seminar at major conventions, and to writer's associations in person and on Zoom. Everything I shared in these sessions is included in this book, and more.

People have hired me to promote their books, but I've given that up. Instead, I now ask them to buy this book which is way cheaper than my old fee. You win and I don't lose that much. All this is to show you that I'm on your side. I want you to sell lots of copies of your book. And I want to create the conditions that make it an attractive prospect for adaptation.

My advice is geared toward un-agented authors like me, self-published authors, and even those published by the Big Five who are shocked at how little the company budgeted to promote their book. We have lots to discuss, but first I'd like to begin with a story…

"MY WORDS WILL SELL THEMSELVES. EVENTUALLY."

Recently, I read a book by a friend who attended one of my "DIY Book Promo" sessions. I was looking for new examples deserving all-out promotion and this novel ticked all the boxes.

The prose? Brilliant. Compelling characters and airtight plot? Check and check. Cover art to pop out of any shelf or online listing? You'll learn just how effective in a moment. My friend was ready to tap into the huge and hungry market for romance novels, and Valentine's Day was just around the corner.

Those at her book launch said all the things an author would want to hear, including several admitting how much they wanted to fuck that book cover. Perhaps more revealing was an animated discussion about which Hollywood A-listers should play the main characters. Looking around the room, I knew immediately this book was fire. The only thing needed was a sustained push by its author. I hoped to hear more about her strategy and success when we met for coffee three weeks later.

"So, how did your book do for Valentine's Day?"

She shrugged. "It did okay."

When I pressed, she revealed only a dozen copies sold. "And that's fine," she waved. "My words will sell themselves. Eventually."

I kept it upbeat. "Spring break's coming up. People want a book for the beach, right? Rum drink, cabana, romance novel." I pointed. "There's your next campaign."

"I know you're trying to help, Dan, but I'm not a publicist. Can't an author just be an author?"

I winced. It's hard to watch another literary achievement wilt because the author couldn't bother to pick it up and move it into the sunshine. I didn't say this to my friend, and perhaps I should've, but I'll say it to you: The only books that sell themselves are penned by celebrities. If you're not famous, you will need a chief marketer. And nobody knows a book better than its author. Before we proceed, however, I need to check in with you.

What's the goal for your book? Is it something you want to share only with family and friends? Okay, thanks for reading to this point. There's no reason to stay because my advice won't help. If you're looking for thousands of readers or would love to see your book adapted into another medium, I can help—unless you're rich and can pay for publicity. If this is you, I don't expect you to stay but I hope you'll give this book to someone willing to do the work. All set? Here's my preliminary list of what you'll need:

1. **A book you really believe in**. It must be your best work, or equal to your best. If you aren't 100% confident in what you wrote, no one else will be.

2. **Blogger reviews**. Here I mean reviews beyond the ones your friends leave on Goodreads. Pitch bloggers who specialize in your genre. They've read everyone who came before you (or nearly

everyone) so their reviews have credibility. They will be tougher, though, so adjust your hopes to four stars instead of five. Four from a blogger is very good. If you get this score, you'll have further evidence that your book is worth promoting.

3. **More engagement on social media**. Instagram, TikTok, Facebook—each appeals to different demographics, and they offer different ways to find readers. Their algorithms present a united front, however, in suppressing anything that resembles promotion. Still, keep this in mind: Those same algorithms are tuned to recognize relevance. They aim to increase the platform's popularity, so boosting your relevance will automatically increase your reach. Find a way to make that happen, even if it's in a Facebook group or a community gathered around a hashtag. Start small and build from there.

4. **More events**. Bookstore and library appearances are well-known for delivering little return on investment. Most of us have experienced the disappointment of selling few, if any, copies at a book signing. But the event itself isn't the goal. It's the hook for what you're really going after...

STEP UP TO THE MIC

"What did you have for breakfast today?"

This is the first question I asked people who came to be interviewed at WNIJ, the NPR station where I had an author interview program. This always-unexpected query immediately prompted a Proustian reverie starring a bagel, cup of coffee, or bacon and eggs. No madeleines appeared, but even the most nervous guest looked and sounded relaxed after declaiming the morning menu. The result was a recording that was more conversation than Q & A, something that engaged listeners and boosted the confidence of my guest. I hope you have a similar experience when you go on radio, TV, or a podcast to promote your book.

Not everyone is comfortable speaking into a microphone and I'm sure introverts are quivering as they read this. Nevertheless, we both know interviews are necessary if you want to reach a wider audience so...take time to breathe while I recommend the best avenues to pitch.

At first glance, changes in "legacy" media appear to present fewer opportunities for authors. No doubt you've heard that local news outlets keep getting acquired by private equity firms and conglomerates. To save money, the new owners almost always cut newsroom staff. As a result, the remaining reporters struggle to cover the city council or school board, so any author pitching their book can expect a frazzled response — if they get one at all.

In this landscape, public radio stations remain an oasis. Many of these have teamed up with Report for America which works to stem the proliferation of news deserts. RfA partially funds reporters covering a variety of beats so check if your local station has an arts or feature reporter and find ways to connect with them. Another medium that keeps expanding is podcasts, and many well-known personalities are migrating to this newer platform. Ditto for streaming stations.

Despite my earlier gloomy words about legacy media, some communities are fortunate to still have locally owned AM and FM stations and newspapers. And some TV stations continue devoting an hour to interesting people and happenings in their community. Be sure to check for these when you schedule an event.

It may seem obvious, but I cannot stress this enough if you're invited to an interview: Be on time and prepared. Check the address and driving distance and leave extra time for traffic or weather. If it's a virtual interview, make sure your family members stay out of sight and earshot. Check your lighting and background, plus appearance. Also, know how you'll respond to basic questions like what inspired your book. Many interviewers will only have time to read the back cover synopsis, so you'll probably be asked to describe the book during the recording. I recommend limiting your description to thirty seconds, which may take practice. If the interviewer wants more, they'll ask. And when it comes to reading an excerpt make sure you rehearse a few times before going live. This goes for in-person events too. Nothing bores an audience like a reader mumbling, chin down, while stumbling through their words. And for the love of God, don't read from your phone. Print some pages instead.

During your reading, raise your head and make eye contact now and then. Reading aloud is a performance and you're there to close the deal with book buyers. If you're uncomfortable doing this in public, try practicing in front of a friend or on video. As a last resort borrow this trick attributed to Winston Churchill who, legend has it, vanquished his fear of public speaking by imagining his audience in their underwear.

When deciding who to interview, hosts and editors often look for certain topics or genres with a seasonal hook. If you wrote a horror story, October is the obvious time. A beach read begs for June. And any story set during Thanksgiving or Christmas has a built-in audience. Just make sure you send your pitch at least a month beforehand.

Checking back with our introvert friends...How are you doing? Feeling ready? Here's a tip for flipping the script when the recording starts: Be the first to ask, "So what did you have for breakfast today?" It's a great way to break the ice. If you're facing an inexperienced reporter, they might feel steadier after answering. You'll create a trusting space for both of you and the interview should go smoothly.

Extra points if their response includes the madeleine that always eluded me. Now lean toward the mic — but not too close — and knock 'em dead.

***

A final note: Make sure you get a recording of the interview or know where to find it. Then share on all your platforms. And when pitching other media outlets, include a link to your highest profile interview up to that point. Make yourself the story everyone wants to chase!

ABOUT YOUR TIME

During my campaign for Fiona's Guardians, I wrote hardly any fiction. I published some articles, but most of my waking hours went to promoting my novel. For me, writing fiction is a deeper dive requiring more imagination and focus. I also knew the sequel would need time to marinate. And besides, nobody will buy a follow-up book if they haven't read the first one, right? So, I threw myself into marketing. This included many hours in Facebook groups devoted to fans of vampires, Dracula, and gothic horror. I also researched book bloggers and other reviewers. Weeks into my campaign, I questioned whether I was a writer anymore. I did, however, take some comfort knowing that pitch emails, social media posts, and captions still involved the careful selection of words.

Should you adopt a similar approach? Depends on what your goals are. My book's breakthrough moments resulted from seeds planted many months earlier. And there were several high points that I'll get to. However, I need to acknowledge some realities that may require you to adjust this strategy to fit your life.

Are you working full-time? Consider making promotion a part-time job of 3-4 hours a day, including weekends. If you have a young child, an ill parent, or are coping with a chronic condition, try to reserve an hour a day or even 30 minutes. With this schedule, you'll need to be more targeted about which bookstores or libraries to pitch, how many Facebook groups you'll participate in, and what events you can commit to. Just make sure to get the most from whatever time you can spare. Your book deserves it. And if you keep pushing – a little every day – you will move the needle. People will read your book and tell their friends and followers. The ripple effect will take longer to spread, but this isn't a race. You're the only one you're competing against, so enjoy the process of promoting your book when time allows.

ABOUT YOUR MONEY

The subtitle of this book is "How to find readers without spending money," and I've tried hard to stick to this brief. For example, I'll never advise you to pay for a boost on social media or an ad in a newspaper. If you decide to do either, I hope it's worth it. However, I must draw the line at paying for an interview. Respectable media outlets consider this a violation of professional integrity, and I agree 100%. Besides, we're authors, right? Nobody should expect us to have money for any of the above. In that spirit, this book will presume your marketing budget is zero.

But what about a website, Dan? Isn't that an important tool that costs money? Yes, probably, although I need to point out there's some debate about whether an author really needs one. I'll err on the side that says a website is a good investment for those who are relatively unknown. This, of course, leads to the matter of paying to reserve a domain name. I think we'll all agree that nobody wants a cyber squatter buying YourName.com and holding it hostage. Reserving and protecting your domain name for a year or three may also be tax deductible. What's more,

YourName.com could also be useful for selling merchandise other than books.

When it comes to building your site, there are free options. I know of at least one web builder that doesn't charge anything if you use a URL they provide. If you want to transfer YourName.com to this site, you'll need to upgrade to a package that costs a few dollars a month. Any tax deduction in this case will be more complicated since a website is regarded as a capital asset. Expect to deduct over time, not all at once.

Of course, certain expenses are inevitable if you travel to an event but some of these, like food and fuel, may be tax-deductible. Professional development also falls into this category, so you may be able to deduct conference admission fees. If you have any questions about anything tax related, consult a certified public accountant or CPA.

When it comes to ordering books for events, you'll want to obtain them at the lowest possible price. Most bookstores take 40% commission so we're trying to break even while keeping our eye on the prize (media interviews).

Okay, time for a show of hands. How many authors order their supplies from Amazon? I see a lot of you out there, which should surprise no one. The Prime discount with fast, free delivery is something many publishers can't match for author copies. If you print via Kindle Direct Publishing (KDP), your profit margin will likely be higher. Unfortunately, some bookstores reject Amazon authors because sales benefit their biggest competitor. Other booksellers are happy to take the standard 40% no matter where the book comes from, so never hesitate to ask.

Some aspects of marketing have a value that's difficult to quantify. This includes photos and videos of your book with booksellers, fans, and even celebrities. The same goes for a high-quality interview. These will be powerful tools as you promote your book, and you can use them forever.

Finally, it costs nothing to pitch bookstores for an event. I will talk a lot about indie bookshops in this book because they're more likely to stock books by local authors. Also, they – like all mom-and-pop shops -- have something I call the "halo effect." Co-branding with them will allow you benefit from that shine. But when should you pitch these stores, and what should your email include? Follow me to the next chapter.

THE INVITATION

If you shop at your local indie bookstore, and your friends have ordered your book from them, you're well-placed to get an invitation. But a pitch email is a good reminder when they're looking for authors that fit with certain holidays or national celebrations like Juneteenth or Pride Month. Keep your email simple. It should include your name, the book's title, ISBN number, and – most importantly -- a review. If you're angling for a certain month, make sure your pitch arrives two months prior. That should give the store plenty of time to organize an event they believe will attract the most customers.

Naturally, they are hoping you will bring new shoppers through their door. So, make sure you're active on social media when you pitch them. Few things are more discouraging to a bookseller than an author who hasn't posted for a couple of months.

When the invitation arrives, announce it immediately on all your platforms, tagging the bookstore. Now start composing your pitches to local media. Hopefully, you've researched who to contact at the newspapers, TV stations, AM/FMs, and any podcasters with a local focus. What should this email look like? Keep it short and friendly.

They'll want to know who you are, where and when your event happens, and why anyone should care. Again, it helps a great deal if your book has a seasonal hook or fits in with, say, St. Patrick's Day or Asian American Month. Hot topics are another way to get the attention of a producer or editor. These include triumphing over trauma, homeschooling, and local lore or history. Near the bottom of your email, drop a link to a review and offer up a free e-copy of your book.

Next, compose emails to the chamber of commerce and downtown association. I usually copy and paste my media pitch and then replace the interview request for a mention in their Facebook page or newsletter. Also, there's no need to offer a free book but keep the review link.

If none of the respondents get back to you and it's 7-10 days before the event, you could send private messages to their Facebook pages. Some media outlets monitor these closely for news tips, but not all. I must warn you, though: Sending too many private messages could get your account frozen or even suspended – and that's the last thing you need before your event. So, proceed with caution.

Here's something else to think about: Don't hesitate to approach bookstores outside your community. If you have family in another state, you're a local author there, too. And you have a place to stay. Driving your own car could be cost-effective, especially if you can get to their house within a day. Still, the cost of an airline ticket might be worth the time you spend with family. Whichever mode you choose, my advice remains the same re: interviews. It's well worth the time researching out-of-state media outlets because scoring an interview there will introduce your book to a whole new audience. Plus, you'll have further proof that your book has legs.

Allow me to recount a crazy, hastily organized book tour I did in July 2023. At the beginning of the month, Wisconsin Public Radio invited me on to talk about vampire myths and lore. The program was meant to highlight midwestern authors in this genre, but I'd just moved from northern Illinois to Kentucky. The producer didn't mind, and we went ahead as scheduled.

Vampire myths and lore from Midwestern novelists

Air Date: Monday, July 10, 2023, 8:00am

SHARE: ✉ 📘

▶ Listen ⊙ Download

Since before Bram Stoker conjured up "Dracula" in 1897, vampire fiction has endured in the blood-drained hearts of horror fans. We're joined by three Midwestern writers who embrace the genre but put their own spin on the ghastly allure of vampirism.

Host(s):
Kate Archer Kent
Guest(s):
Jacqueline Holland
Dan Klefstad
Scott Burtness

Because this was a statewide program, I wrote to every bookstore in Wisconsin, alerting them to the date and time of the interview, then wrote to them afterward to share the link. I was hoping a few shops would order my book for stock. What I didn't expect was an invitation, but that's what I got. OtherWorlds Books in Sturgeon Bay asked me to participate in a multi-author event during a city-wide sidewalk sale. That was in two weeks, and I lived 500 miles away. Fortunately, I'd just retired so, why not?

To make this work, I phoned a dozen or so booksellers in eastern Wisconsin, trying to string together a mini tour. Two more agreed to host me, all within three hours' driving distance. My sister-in-law who lives in Wisconsin saw my Facebook posts about this and offered her family's lake house which I gratefully accepted. In the end, I spent as much on gas and food as I earned in sales. But I got great pics from Lyons Fine Books in Neenah, and Reader's Realm in Montello. Plus, I appeared in a video promoting the Sturgeon Bay event. Was all this worth the trip? I still have the mentality that I'm winning readers one at a time, so yeah.

But enough about me. Let's plan your event.

Ready for your book signing?

Hopefully, you alerted your followers and the bookstore (or library) alerted theirs. If you were lucky enough to get in the local paper or on the radio, be sure to share this news with the venue as well as your social media pages. On the big day, know when you walk through the door you probably sold more copies because of the interview than you'll sell on site, and that's okay. Stay upbeat. Be friendly to the customers even if they're not interested in your book and be especially nice to the manager and staff. Before you leave, ask if they want autographed copies for customers who missed the event.

Figure 1 With Arlene Lynes, owner of Read Between the Lynes bookstore in Woodstock, Illinois.

Here's another item you'll need: photos and videos. Ask a staffer to hold your book for the camera. On social media, few things get better engagement than a smiling bookseller giving a thumbs-up to your title and cover art. After all, readers look to these folks for recommendations. Bonus points if you get your book pictured with the resident cat or dog; they are engagement gold. Be sure to post these often, occasionally tagging the bookstore so they know you're promoting them.

Figure 2 Feline booksellers Huck & Finn, courtesy of From My Shelf Books and Gifts in Wellsboro, Pennsylvania.

Now that I've beguiled you with #catpics, I'll address the mundane topic of logistics. As the author of a vampire novel, late September to Halloween is when I'm busiest. I typically schedule book signings every weekend and bring my own copies as part of a consignment deal (60% for the author is usual). During this period, I'm constantly watching my stock of books to make sure I have enough. If a store manager orders copies anticipating a big turnout, I never worry about the event being a flop. Why? Because I always need extras. At the end of a slow day, I'll ask the manager to sell me the remainders at cost.

If you didn't get on local media and worry the event will be a waste of time, you could cancel. Only do this if you're sure the store didn't order copies. If they're stuck with books they can't return, they'll never invite you again. Also, give them at least two days' notice.

***

No doubt, you've noticed the importance I attach to good reviews that essentially serve as your calling card. If you're wondering who you should approach for a review, I can help, but be prepared for my unpopular opinion on who not to pitch. I maintain that nothing is more important than ensuring all reviews are trustworthy. Follow me to the next chapter where we'll raise the bar.

TO PAY OR NOT TO PAY

You've seen the ads offering reviews from publications with long authoritative histories. One well-known outlet reviews books by established authors who pay no fee. But explore the site and you'll learn that indie authors must spend hundreds of dollars to attach this company's brand to their book. And it's a powerful brand. Of course, such reviews are always presented as honest, and maybe they are. But how can we be sure when there's a clear conflict of interest? The company could've addressed this by making it easy to see books with unflattering remarks – effectively saying, "Money can buy lots of things but not an impartial review!" Instead, they did the opposite. They allow authors to keep bad reviews unpublished. As a result, visitors to the site are likely to see only favorable reviews purchased by authors.

Have we forgotten who we're working for? It's one thing to challenge a reader with, say, experimental prose. It's another to sell them something when you're not being 100% transparent. The trustworthiness of all reviews is at stake here, so let me propose a solution: include language *in the review* stating that the author paid for this service. And the review, favorable or not, gets published. If you have a better, fairer way to inform the consumer, I'm all ears.

Compare the above to how book bloggers operate. Here I'm talking about amateur reviewers who read multiple genres and set up their sites mainly to remember books. They don't charge the author and clearly disclose *in the review* when they receive a free copy of the book. That's five stars for ethics! Another plus: They're very active on social media. A typical blogger has thousands of followers, and all have an enviable list of subscribers. True, many participate in blog tours which charge authors a fee, and some offer paid publicity services. But their free reviews are above reproach. Sure, they lack a fancy brand and, yes, they gush like teenagers when a book excites them. But is that bad? If they love you, they'll shout your name from the rooftops. Bathe in their praise without shame.

It's publication day for **Fiona's Guardians** by Dan Klefstad and I am delighted to be reviewing the book in celebration. Happy publication day, Dan, and my thanks for the digital copy of your book, which I have reviewed honestly and impartially.

Figure 3 Screenshot from the blog, A Little Book Problem, which reviewed Fiona's Guardians on Oct. 2, 2020.

At the beginning of this book, I mentioned another type of blogger who specializes in genres like horror, sci fi, or fantasy. These reviewers serve aficionados. A good review here will get the attention of your core audience. However, it's worth noting that these bloggers are not well networked outside the genre, so it'll be up to you to share their review. For this, you'll need an important tool.

A ROLODEX BY ANOTHER NAME

Frustrated with social media? Ready to deactivate your accounts and say, "good riddance!" to the bots that limit your posts? I feel your pain but keep your accounts for now. A little further down, I'll suggest ways to boost your relevance, which is what those pesky algorithms are looking for. First, I'd like you to travel back with me to the 1990s when email was all the rage (after grunge rock and side ponytails). As I write this, in 2023, an email list remains a powerful tool to reach your audience. And having an easy way to capture addresses is crucial. Let's have a look at your website. Does it have a button allowing visitors to subscribe to your blog or newsletter? Or maybe you have a contact page that sends messages to your email. That's another way to add an address, but I recommend asking those who send a comment or question if they'd like future messages about your events, publishing news, etc.

I have several email lists divided into local/regional media, national media, book bloggers, plus one I call "Your Readers." The biggest by far, though, is reserved for independent bookstores in the U.S., Canada, and the U.K. Remember at the beginning when I said my novel, Fiona's Guardians, joined the inventory of dozens of bookstores?

This is the result of thousands of emails I sent to shops that carry new books. You see, rather than commit to a weekly or monthly blog or newsletter, I devoted enormous amounts of time researching retailers, then pitching my novel (with a link to a review). Most of these shops I've never visited. And yet, *and yet*, a small percentage wrote back to say they ordered one or two copies for their shelves. Immediately, I thanked them and asked for photos, preferably with a staffer holding my book. Several opted to send display pics, which was disappointing because these get less engagement. But many did send what I asked for and I continue to share these on all my platforms. And now let's return to the topic of relevance.

Posting a pic or video of a smiling bookseller holding your book will attract plenty of likes, comments, and even shares. Expect double the engagement if it's a #bookstorecat posted on #caturday or #happycaturday. Seriously, make it your goal to acquire this content, or something else floofy and cute like #bookstoredog. The more reactions you get, the more relevant your post becomes, and the more relevant you will become.

Another way to attract algorithmic love is posting in a Facebook group that resonates with your genre. Every day, post a meme, comment, or share information that keeps the conversation going. Increasing your visibility will prompt others to tag you, seek your opinion, and share with other groups. Facebook wins by scooping up more information it can sell advertisers, and you win when the algorithms partner with you during your search for book buyers.

If you're thinking, "This sounds creepy," keep in mind that users understand the deal they made when they signed up for their free account. They keep participating because it's an easy way to find folks who share their passions. If you want to sell books, you'll need to join these conversations because finding them IRL can be a lot harder.

PUT ON A SHOW!

Sometime during my campaign, I realized my novel had a much higher Goodreads score than 'Salem's Lot by Stephen King. I saw an opportunity to link my vampire novel to Mr. King's and wondered if this could make a splash. So, I released a YouTube video in which I challenged the world's best-known horror author to push his followers to boost the rating for his book. Next, I shared this video with a YouTube horror channel, and -- to my surprise -- the host led his next episode with my challenge.

Figure 4 Mr. Deadman, host of Horror Talk Radio

After this episode of Horror Talk Radio, I tried to keep the ball rolling by pitching several newspapers. One in England, the Biggleswade Chronicle, picked up the story. My publisher was based in the paper's coverage area at the time, so I used that angle in my pitch. One of their reporters interviewed me, which allowed me to say more about my book.

People

Shefford vampire novel is ratings rival for horror legend Stephen King

Author Dan Klefstad reveals the secrets of what it's like working for a beautiful, manipulative vampire - and her penchant for O Negative!

By Joanna Gravett
Published 7th Jul 2021, 14:26 GMT
Updated 8th Jul 2021, 15:48 GMT

Of course, I shared this article across the universe, which led to more views of the Horror Talk Radio video and more sales of my book. Unfortunately, the national outlets ignored this story because Mr. King didn't respond. So, it died after a couple weeks. But what a brief and wondrous life it had. You can still find my original video, plus the Horror Talk Radio one, on YouTube.

Since then, the rating for my novel has sunk closer to King's, which I expected. The law of averages practically guarantees that more ratings will, over time, lower your score. So, if you plan to copy my stunt, do it when your book is still fresh.

Sometimes, opportunities plunk down right in front of you. In November of 2023, Scottish actor Graham McTavish toured my hometown of Louisville, Kentucky, to promote his new line of whiskey. One of his stops was a retailer ten minutes from my house. In case you don't know, Mr. McTavish starred in the Outlander TV series, plus the Hobbit movies. He also voices Dracula in the anime series Castlevania, so I thought that would be a nice tie-in for my novel. At the venue, I greeted McTavish with the usual praises and presented an inscribed hardcover edition of my book as a gift. Incredibly, he agreed to pose holding my book.

Minutes after posting this, my Facebook and Instagram accounts blew up with comments and reactions. Aligning my book with such star power increased my relevance for several days, but I'm pinning my hopes on something bigger: Perhaps Mr. McTavish reads my book and likes it. Would he ask one of his people to approach me about a film or streaming adaptation? The answer is probably no, but who am I to say? All I knew was his appearance at my local liquor store deserved my best shot (pardon the pun). If I get nothing else, I have an amazing photo.

GET YOUR BOOK ADAPTED

This may prove difficult, but it is possible, so you need to try. As with many things, opportunities arise in unexpected places.

On the Saturday before Labor Day, 2021, seven union actors walked into a studio to record a podcast adaptation of my novel. They'd been struggling to find work ever since theaters closed due to COVID-19. During the pandemic, some acting companies started what I'll call "theater of the mind" podcasts to keep actors working and reach new audiences. Many of these resemble radio plays from the 1930s. One company, Artists' Ensemble Theater or AET, specializes in adaptations of Agatha Christie novels which entered the public domain. I was familiar with them, and they with me, because they produced a couple of plays for WNIJ, the radio station where I worked. One of their players was a midday host at WNIJ, and he suggested I meet with AET's producing director, Richard Raether. I called him to pitch an adaptation of my novel, and he seemed reluctant, citing an already heavy schedule for their Mysterious Journey podcast. I sent him the novel anyway. A few weeks later, I got an email from his wife Margaret, the resident playwright at AET, with a script attached. I knew immediately it was brilliant. The contract involved no money, which was fine because I saw a rare opportunity here.

The Raethers' daughter, Casiena, played the vampire Fiona. She's well-known to Chicago audiences as an actor, singer, and dancer. A regular AET star, David A. Gingerich, played Daniel, Fiona's main guardian. Another fine actor from the Chicago area, Andrew Harth, played Wolf, a guardian-in-training.

It's easy to call me biased, but everyone who listened said it was exceptionally well-done. These included a New York literary agent who gave valuable advice regarding my manuscript before eventually passing on it. You can find the "Fiona's Guardians" episode wherever you get podcasts. Just look under Mysterious Journey.

This AET production made it easier to imagine further adaptations, and I've been working with a director/screenwriter on a short film based on my novel. For this I'm learning how to write a screenplay, which I consider an important skill for any writer. We'll see how it goes...

Figure 5 Casiena Raether who played the vampire Fiona in the Mysterious Journey adaptation of Fiona's Guardians.

So how can you get your work adapted? The first step is to ask. Does your community have a theater company? Have you discovered a podcast that dramatizes works in your genre? Maybe you know a recent graduate from film school who's looking for something different. Whatever the medium, find the decision-makers and ask the question.

One thing they'll consider is how well you've promoted your book. Those who invest in theater, film, and streaming productions need to know what kind of return they can expect. Sales figures for your book will be an important clue.

If you're skeptical about whether it's worth the effort, allow me to point out the things you're missing or dismissing: 1) More people will know about your book if they see the words, "From the novel by…" or "Based on the memoirs of…" 2) You'll have something important to share with your followers. 3) You'll have something important to share with news outlets.

You might've noticed a theme throughout this book, and that's creating conditions to capitalize on the next opportunity. The more you push, the more barriers you'll break through. And keep in mind: I may think I'm special but I'm no more special than you. Plus, you miss 100% of the shots you don't take, so what have you got to lose?

"NOTHING DOING? GET CREDENTIALED!"

When you're high, it's easy to forget about the inevitable crash. This chapter is about that difficult transition many feel after going flat-out for weeks. You've traveled from event to event, speaking to media, posing with fans, and selling lots of copies. Then everything grinds to a halt. Maybe your book's "season" has ended (November can be an awful hangover for horror writers). Or perhaps your hot topic has been eclipsed by a new, hotter one. Media love is famously fickle, and your book sales will reflect those "on again" and "off again" moments.

A sudden lack of activity might be welcome to those needing a break. I, however, am constantly fretting about the readers I'm not reaching. Wherever you are on this spectrum, it's best to remember the things we can't control. For example, hardly anyone buys a book in January; they're reading what they received as gifts during the holidays.

Many use the lean months to write their next book, which seems a wise choice. If, however, you want to keep the ball rolling, ask yourself what you haven't done. Try looking in the mirror. Do you see an expert there? During your campaign you probably developed strong opinions about writing, publishing, or marketing. You might even have something controversial to say about your genre. If you're not sure about this, or have impostor syndrome, let me point out that authors typically make more money from presentations than from book sales – and many of them know little more than you do. Is that enough to push aside any self-doubt? Let's burnish your credentials.

It starts with an article. Compose a compelling argument that lends a fresh view to existing knowledge or dares to say something new. After edits and revisions, let's consider where to publish it. You could put it on your blog and share from there. But I'll suggest pitching it to a journal, industry blog, or any site where an editor decides what gets published. This is not a slight against those who self-publish. Self-publishing continues to be a legitimate path for novels and memoirs. Becoming an expert, however, is a different matter. Getting past a gatekeeper will show that at least one professional believes in you. That's all you'll need.

This book began as an article I submitted to the Chicago Writers Association's blog in 2021. The editor added it to their collection of essays about various aspects of the writing life. My "DIY Book Promo" piece became the blueprint for a PowerPoint I still present at book fairs and conventions.

So, Expert, where should you apply? Start with book festivals. The larger ones have slots that fill up quickly, so submit your application as early as possible. And don't worry about your presentation being a good fit for the event. That's for the organizers to decide. Author guilds or writer's associations present another opportunity. Many of them invite speakers from outside the group to share their expertise. Just make sure you know how to share your PowerPoint or other media on Zoom.

Getting a speaking engagement will raise your profile among your peers and followers. It's also another arrow in your quiver when pursuing media interviews. Get enough gigs and the media will start calling you. It's a great feeling when that happens. Here's hoping you remain in the spotlight for as long as possible. And when your star power wanes, as it inevitably will, something important – something you might almost have forgotten -- will be waiting for you: Your next book. Before we get to that, however, I need to address some FAQs.

MY PITCH

Throughout these chapters I've yammered on about the importance of pitch letters, and you might be wondering if I'd provide examples. Let me give you two I sent announcing this book to media outlets. The first went out when DIY Book Promo opened for pre-orders in February 2024. The subject line -- Local author aims to help writers find readers w/out spending $$ -- changed to "Kentucky author" or "Midwest native," depending on the recipient:

Greetings. My new book, DIY Book Promo: How to Find Readers without Spending Money, is available for preorder. The Feb. 28 release is timed to coincide with speaking engagements I have on this topic -- including at the Imaginarium Convention.

DIY Book Promo incorporates lessons from my 30-year radio career, plus the three-year marketing campaign for my novel, Fiona's Guardians. In it, I share all my tools and tricks so fellow authors can connect with readers while avoiding paid publicity services and scammers who prey on the millions of writers who just want their work to be remembered.

Have a look at my website below my signature. I'll be happy
to say more in an interview.

Thanks for your consideration,
Dan K
--
Dan Klefstad
http://www.diybookpromo.com
July 19-21 at the Imaginarium Convention, Louisville, KY

Nothing fancy, just short and to the point, with my
upcoming speaking engagements as the hook. The follow-
up letter ramped up the attention-getting. It divided my
pitch into elements, starting with the subject line (The
problem: Millions of authors waste $$ on paid promo
services). The body of the email picks up immediately
where the subject line left off:

My solution: DIY Book Promo: How to Find Readers without
Spending Money

"Never pay for publicity again," is the mantra of yours truly,
an author and longtime radio host. In my new book, DIY Book
Promo, I share the tools and tricks I learned during my 30-year
broadcast career plus the three-year marketing campaign for
my novel, Fiona's Guardians. I'll show how to use free
resources to reach readers, placing a strong emphasis on
obtaining media interviews, performing well in front of the
mic, and co-branding with indie bookstores.

News hook: The release of DIY Book Promo coincides with
speaking engagements I have on this topic, including at the
Imaginarium Convention this summer.

Let's get together via phone or Zoom. If I can drive to your
studio, I will. Let's help the hundreds -- perhaps thousands --
of writers in your market who are trying hard to find their
readers.

Sincere regards,

Dan K
--
Dan Klefstad
http://www.diybookpromo.com
July 19-21 at the Imaginarium Convention, Louisville, KY

In both emails, I attached the cover art for my book. As of this writing, I'm drafting a third round of emails, closer to some of the events I've scheduled. If a fourth is needed, I'll send one. Hopefully the examples I provided will help you compose a brief, focused pitch.

If you have one that worked for you, please share with me via email or at the next conference or festival.

LICKING YOUR WOUNDS

I get a lot of questions about moving past rejection, so I'll address that here. If you haven't been rejected numerous times, I'd question whether you actually queried an agent or publisher, or pitched a bookstore, reviewer, or anyone in this business. As for me, I've been rejected hundreds of times – including this very morning by the head of a major book festival in Florida. I'd pitched myself as a speaker on book marketing and she replied, "Thanks for writing but my authors that come in are all NYT best sellers, so they are well aware of how to promote."

Ouch.

My first rejection letters arrived in 2015 when I pitched a manuscript for a fictional memoir about a single mother who suffered trauma in the army. After many months of "Thanks, but no thanks," I finally got my first publishing contract. Then I realized I'd need some reviews, so I sent another round of emails to bloggers. Their verdicts couldn't have been more varied, ranging from "Unconventional and refreshing" to "It read like the ramblings of a crazy woman and for a short amount of time that's fine but not for 267 pages!"

Despite some enthusiastic write-ups, the book sold hardly any copies, prompting the publisher to let me go. When I pitched my next novel to them, I got this reply:

"Sorry, Dan, but we are not moving ahead as your publisher."

I am living proof that bad reviews and rejection letters will make you stronger -- if you let them. One of the people who inspired me is not a writer, but a freelance IT worker featured on NPR's *Invisibilia* podcast. His name is Jason Comley, a thirty-something who spiraled into depression and paranoia after his wife left him. She found someone who was taller and wealthier than he was. Comley's feelings about himself got so bad that he became afraid to leave the house and meet new people. In his words: "I had nowhere to go, and no one to hang out with... so I just broke down and started crying." Comley realized he was afraid, so he asked himself: afraid of what?

"I'm afraid of rejection," he realized.

Comley resolved to get over his fear. He decided to make a game out of rejection, and this is pretty much what I've done. Comley made a point of getting rejected at least once every day. After a while, it felt good to get rejected all the time because, as Comley put it: "I disobeyed fear."

Disobeyed. Comley really hit on something there. I'd never thought that fear depended on our obedience, but it does. When you consider this, it's easy to conclude that rejection is really an empty threat.

So how does a published author play Comley's rejection game? You pitch reviewers, news editors, bookstores, or book festivals. When a bad review comes in, remember this: Your book isn't pizza. Pitch someone else. Any serious reviewer who takes the time to bash you in public has at least taken the time to read your work. Someday, years from now, they'll encounter you at a conference or online forum, and they'll see you survived them. You kept writing, despite their criticism, and managed to find an audience and build on it. When they realize they couldn't keep you down, they'll have no choice but to respect you – however grudgingly.

The same holds true for media professionals who ignore you, bookstores that refuse to stock you, and, yes, festivals that decline your request to speak or sit on a panel. The fact that you're still standing should be enough to make every gatekeeper question their judgement.

Feel better now? Enough to keep going? Good. Let's move on.

YOUR NEXT BOOK

You've pushed your book out as far as it can go (at least for now). You've raised your profile as high as you can (again, for now). You've tried every trick included in this book and others. It's time to ask if you have another book in you. If the answer is yes, go all-in just like you did with marketing.

During the period when you compose in isolation, know you are not alone. I promised my readers (and my publisher) a sequel to Fiona's Guardians and am about to resume work on that. If you're looking for tips on writing an unputdownable book, there are plenty of resources out there, including experienced authors who make a living hosting workshops online, and at festivals and conventions.

As for me, I have ideas about what makes a good story, and I might position myself as an expert on this someday. But aren't you tired of me yet? Seriously, get out there and meet more of your peers, especially those who've been around longer than me. You'll learn a lot from these folks.

If you insist on one bit of advice from yours truly, here it is: If any part of your manuscript bores you, trust your gut. It's boring and needs to be improved or eliminated.

When your book is ready, feel free to contact my publisher. Burton Mayers Books puts out quality titles and their contract is author-friendly. Have a look, it's on their front page. Also, the head guy there, Richard Mayers, is wonderful to work with.

Whichever publisher you choose, I wish you the very best as, once again, you set out in search of readers. Hopefully, I've made it clear that this process is a journey with lots of stops but no tangible destination. Enjoy the ride. If our paths cross, I hope we both have time to sit down and swap stories. I'll be especially glad to know if my advice helped you sell lots of books.

Battle speech before I go…

Some mornings, not spilling coffee or breaking a fried egg yolk can seem like a momentous victory. We've all had weeks filled with rejection letters, bad reviews, and feeling ghosted by the media. For courage, some of us start the day with a prayer. I start each day with a war cry:

Rouse yourselves my fellow scribes, my creatives! For the enemy is close at hand -- an invisible hand that delights in obscuring the fruit of our travails. Begone subterfuge! Thy algorithms are but a paper tiger whose tail we'll twist to our advantage. But that's not all. Today we lay siege to the town criers who ignored our repeated pleas for one kind mention. They will rue the day our petitions went unheeded. But wait! The clouds do part and o'erhead I spy battlements erected to deny us the hallowed arena. Be they warned we will knock them asunder so that good citizens gathered for their daily entertainments will at last know our worthy creations. My fellow warriors, the time has come to raise our quills and seize our destiny. Onward to respect! To fame! And may your legacy be everlasting. ARE YOU WITH ME!!!

Whew, I'm stoked, how about you? Ready to sell your book? Don't waste any more time with me. Get out there and promote!

ABOUT THE AUTHOR

Dan Klefstad wrote the vampire novel Fiona's Guardians, which is now also available in hardcover. He is currently writing the sequel which he hopes won't suck (ha, another pun!)

Dan lives in Louisville, Kentucky.